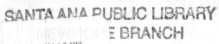
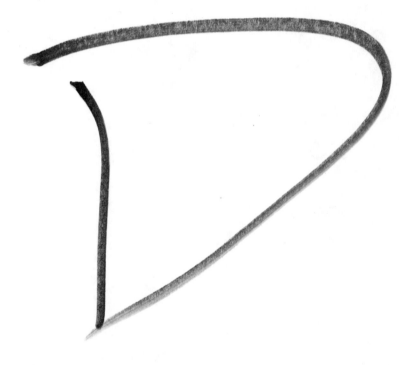

POLICE OFFICERS PROTECT PEOPLE

Design and electronic page composition
Lindaanne Donohoe Design

Photo research
Feldman & Associates, Inc.

● ▲ ● ▼ ● ▲ ● ● ▲ ● ▼ ● ▲ ●

Picture Acknowledgments

©**Lindaanne Donohoe Design** — Cover, 6, 16, 17, 18, 19, 22, 23, 27, 29, 30

David R. Frazier Photolibrary — ©David R. Frazier — 3, 5, 9, 14

©**Phil Martin** — 24, 25, 26

PhotoEdit — ©Michael Newman — 4, 7, 28; ©Tony Freeman — 8;
©Tom Prettyman — 11; ©David Young-Wolff — 12; ©Mary Kate Denny — 21

©**Doug Plummer** — 13

©**David J. Sams** — 10

©**SuperStock International, Inc.** — 15

Unicorn Stock Photos — ©Aneal Vohra — 20

Grateful acknowledgment is made to
the Chicago Police Department
for allowing Ms. Donohoe to photograph police officers at work.

● ▲ ● ▼ ● ▲ ● ● ▲ ● ▼ ● ▲ ●

Library of Congress Cataloging-in-Publication Data

Greene, Carol.

Police officers protect people/Carol Greene.
p.   cm.
Summary: Simple text and photographs describe what police officers do.
ISBN 1-56766-311-7
1. Police — Juvenile literature. 2. Police — United States — Juvenile literature.
[1. Police.] I. Title.

HV7922.G73   1996   96-13839
363.2—dc20   CIP
                                                  AC

CRASH!!!

One car hits another.

Quick. Call the police.

BRR-RING! BRR-RING!

There's been an accident.

No one is hurt, but the drivers are angry.

The dispatcher sends two officers to the scene of the accident. The officers talk to the drivers in two different places.

That way, the drivers can't yell at each other.
"We'll check this out," say the officers.
"You can read our report at the station later."

CLOP! CLOP! CLOP!

An officer and his horse walk through
the park.

This police officer rides
his horse up and down city streets.
CLOP! CLOP!

SWISSSHHH! SWISSSHHH!
An officer on a bicycle rides around an old part of town.

Officers on bikes have special training.
They learn how to cut through
heavy traffic.

They can go places that cars cannot go.
If they have to, they can even ride their
bikes down steps. *BUMPITY! BUMP! ! !*

Most police officers drive police cars.
Sometimes they work by themselves.
Sometimes they work with a partner.

▲▲▲▲▲▲▲▲▲▲▲▲▲▲▲▲▲▲▲▲▲▲▲▲▲▲

When police officers need help
they call for it on their radio.
EEE-OH! EEE-OH! Police cars race to help.

BRRRING! BRRRING!

There's a lost dog
on the school playground.

Police officers don't always catch
lost animals. But this is a special case.
Children could be scared or hurt.

ARF!! ARF!!

An officer catches the dog. She brings it
back to the station and gives it some water.

Then she calls the animal control
people. They will pick up the dog and
look for its owner.

At the high school, police officers are
talking about drugs. Police officers often
work with groups of people.

The dispatcher sends several cars to the
child's home. Many officers have children of
their own. They really care about children.

▲▲▲▲▲▲▲▲▲▲▲▲▲▲▲▲▲▲▲▲▲▲▲▲▲

"Saaaam-my!"

"Saaaam-my!"

The officers search nearby streets.

KNOCK! KNOCK!

They talk to neighbors.

"Have you seen Sammy Smith?"

This officer goes to the playground.

"Have you seen a little boy?" she asks.

"Yes. I saw him over by the park,"
a young boy answers.

The officers have worked for eight hours now.
It's the end of their shift.

They are tired. *WHEW!*

But they are smiling too.

Sammy is home, safe and sound.
Even the lost dog is back with its owners.
The police have done their job.

Questions and Answers

What do police officers do?

Police officers protect people. They make sure everyone obeys the law. They arrest people who break the law. Some officers work with traffic. Others patrol the streets. They try to stop crimes. Many officers help with emergencies, such as fires and accidents.

How do people learn to be police officers?

Police officers have to go to high school. Some then go on to college. They learn about how people behave; they learn about the law. Others go to a police academy for three to six months. New officers work with older ones for a month or two before they go out on their own.

What kind of people are police officers?

Most people who want to be police officers must pass a group of tests first. They are smart and strong. They are healthy and able to work long and hard. And they are brave, because police work can be dangerous. Most of all, police officers care about people and work well with them.

How much money do police officers make?

When officers start their work, they make about $26,000 a year. Later, they make more. A police lieutenant can make more than $38,000 a year. Officers in big cities usually make more than police officers in small towns. But they all do the same job. They help people.

GLOSSARY

accident — something not planned; a mistake

dispatcher — person at the police station who sends police to different places to help people

officer — another name for a policeman or policewoman

partner — a person who works with another person as part of a team

police station — the building that is used by the police to do their work

protecting — keeping something or someone from harm or injury; guarding

radio — a special piece of equipment that carries sounds through the air

report — a paper that puts down all the known facts about something for others to read

scene — the place where something happens

shift — a change from one group of workers to another; when one shift ends, another shift of workers begins

traffic — the number of cars, trucks, and buses passing through a particular place at the same time

training — teaching a special set of skills

▲ ● ▲ ● ▲ ● ▼ ● ▲ ● ▼ ● ▲ ● ▼

CAROL GREENE has written over 200 books for children. She also likes to read books, make teddy bears, work in her garden, and sing. Ms. Greene lives in Webster Groves, Missouri.